DON'T GIVE IN

A **TEEN & ADULT COLORING BOOK**
WITH INSPIRATIONAL QUOTES & SELF-DEVELOPMENT EXERCISES

AVNI PAREKH

The official workbook of award-winning self-help guide,
Be The Bigger Person: Scenarios & Solutions to Better Yourself

DON'T GIVE IN

A Teen & Adult Coloring Book With
Inspirational Quotes & Self-Development Exercises

The official workbook of award-winning self-help guide,
Be The Bigger Person: Scenarios & Solutions to Better Yourself

CONTENTS

CONTENTS

INTRODUCTION

It's easy to lose yourself when you're consumed with pleasing others, living up to professional and personal expectations that have been placed upon you, and not fulfilling your life's purpose.

Don't Give In, is a 31-day, self-development workbook with fill-in-the-blank exercises and inspirational, color-in messages pulled directly from award-winning self-help guide, **Be The Bigger Person: Scenarios & Solutions to Better Yourself.**

The purpose of this transformational workbook and coloring book is two-fold. The first reason is to help you reinforce your self-worth and enable you to reconnect with your authentic self, and the second is to provide you with a therapeutic, emotional release to alleviate stress.

Filled with 31 positive quotes and 31 self-development exercises, the path to self-discovery can take as little as a month's time to outline. The suggested plan is to complete at least one self-development exercise everyday.

To begin, relax your mind by coloring one inspirational message. Then, after you've colored it in, your mind will be at ease so you can start filling out the adjoining exercise which correlates to the quote.

This comprehensive workbook (slash coloring book) will bring you closer to your goals, likes and dislikes, strengths and weaknesses, hobbies, and ultimately – closer to your authentic self.

When you discover who you are and what your purpose is, you're able to live a truly meaningful life.

All my best,
Avni Parekh

AN OATH TO SELF

I, _____ [your name], pledge to do my best to

be the bigger person by taking the high road and not let anger get the best of me, especially when

_____

_____

[list one or more scenarios that could get the better of you].

When I feel like I can't be the bigger person, I will do my best to _____

_____

[describe how will you overcome the urge to act out irrationally].

Additionally, when I am about to succumb to _____

_____

[list one or more emotions or negative behavioral patterns], I will tell myself, "don't give in,"

because that saying will serve as a strong reminder that I have the power to control my mind, urges,

and desires.

Most importantly, I will refer to this self-development workbook to help me gain clarity and

insights into my authentic self.

Date: _____

BE THE BIGGER PERSON | DON'T GIVE IN | BE THE BIGGER PERSON | DON'T GIVE IN

THERE
IS
NO
ONE
LIKE
YOU

Exercise 1: Insights Into Your True Self

Each person is unique in their own way, with a distinct set of experiences, beliefs, and characteristics that make them who they are. To add to that, everybody is on their own personal journey of self-discovery, navigating through the ups and downs of life to find out who they really are and what they stand for. It is through this process of self-discovery that you can truly understand yourself and your place in the world.

Directions: Start to connect with your true self by filling in the blanks below.

1. What are three of your most cherished personal values?
   a. _____
   b. _____
   c. _____

2. What is your purpose in life?
   _____

3. What three words describe you best?
   _____

4. What is your life motto or the philosophy you live by?
   _____

5. What do you wish people understood more about you?
   _____

6. What are your strongest qualities?
   _____

7. What are your weakest qualities?
   _____

8. What would you like to be famous for?
   _____

9. What inspirational quote do you think everyone should hear?
   _____

10. Who do you most admire?
   _____

11. What's one thing that always makes you feel better?
   _____

12. What's the legacy you hope to leave behind?
   _____

Takeaway: We are all on a journey of self discovery. If you seek answers inward, you'll have an opportunity to connect with your authentic and true self. When you connect with your true self, you're able to see your worth and what makes you special.

THE ANSWER LIES WITHIN YOU

Exercise 2: Developing A Positive Self-Image

Cultivating a positive self-image is crucial because it influences our self-esteem, behavior, and the way we communicate with others. A healthy self-image leads to more positive outcomes in life, such as increased confidence and motivation, as well as improved mental and physical health. On the other hand, a negative self-image can lead to low self-esteem, anxiety, depression, and other mental health issues. Therefore, it is vital to prioritize developing and maintaining a positive self-image to live a fulfilling and successful life.

Directions: Write your responses below.

List **5 talents or superpowers** that you possess:

1) _____

2) _____

3) _____

4) _____

5) _____

List **5 characteristics** that you like about yourself:

1) _____

2) _____

3) _____

4) _____

5) _____

List **5 fun facts** about yourself:

1) _____

2) _____

3) _____

4) _____

5) _____

Takeaway: You are one of a kind, always remember that!

THINK GOOD THOUGHTS

Exercise 3: Reclaiming Your Peace Of Mind

It's so important to challenge negative thoughts when they arise. Truth is, negative thoughts are toxic. They create a domino effect of despair that can impact our lives and affect our good mood. Negative thoughts can cause you to perceive situations the wrong way and act out in a manner that makes you appear paranoid and emotionally unstable. That's why it's vital to not only think good thoughts – but to control pessimistic thoughts so they don't spin out of control in your head. There's a saying, hindsight is 20/20. Well, wouldn't it be great to have foresight instead?

Directions: As an example, **think about a situation where a negative thought overtook your peace of mind**. Now, fill in the blanks below.

What happened?

_____

Why did it upset you?

_____

What is the negative thought and how does it make you feel?

_____

How did the situation affect you 5 minutes after it happened? 24 hours? 7 days?

_____

How does that particular situation affect your quality of life?

_____

How much focus are you placing on the negative thought?

_____

Does that negative thought deserve the control it has over you?

_____

When this negative thought pops into your head again, what will you say to yourself so that you don't give in?

_____

Takeaway: When you feel yourself about to react out of anger, review the questions above in your mind to help you battle negative emotions and thoughts.

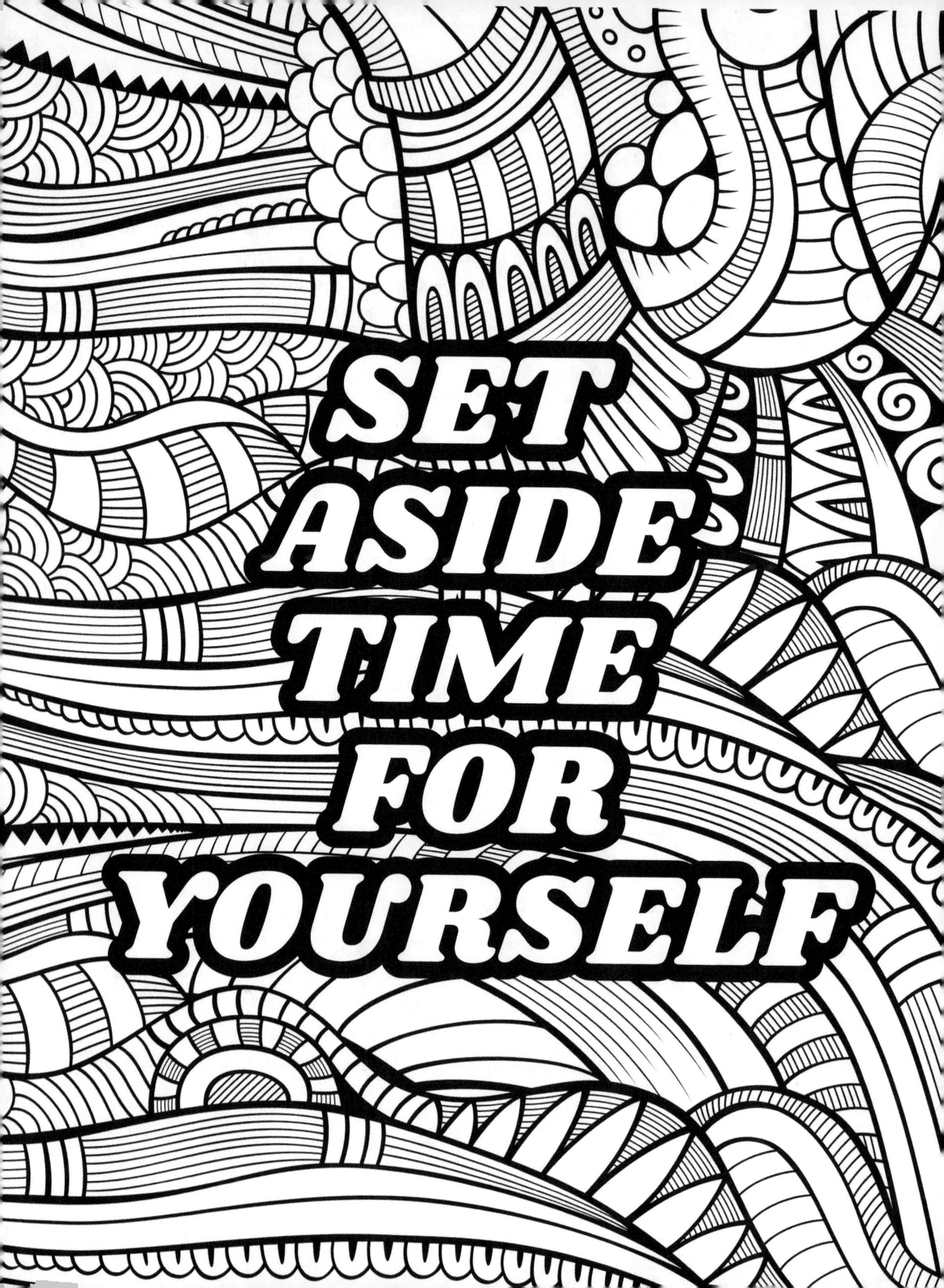
SET
ASIDE
TIME
FOR
YOURSELF

Exercise 4: Making Time For Yourself

Making time for yourself is essential for maintaining good mental and physical health, and reconnecting with your authentic-self. When we constantly prioritize other responsibilities ahead of our own needs, we can become stressed, overwhelmed, and burnt out. Taking time to engage in activities that bring you joy, such as reading a book, going for a walk, or practicing mindfulness, can help reduce stress levels and promote relaxation.

Directions: Write your responses below. Your answers will enable you to make adjustments as needed.

List 5 reasons why you **don't** make time for yourself.

1) _____
2) _____
3) _____
4) _____
5) _____

List 5 reasons why you **need to** make time for yourself.

1) _____
2) _____
3) _____
4) _____
5) _____

List 5 ways you **will** make time for yourself.

1) _____
2) _____
3) _____
4) _____
5) _____

Takeaway: Prioritize making time for yourself; you'll be more present and effective in other areas of life.

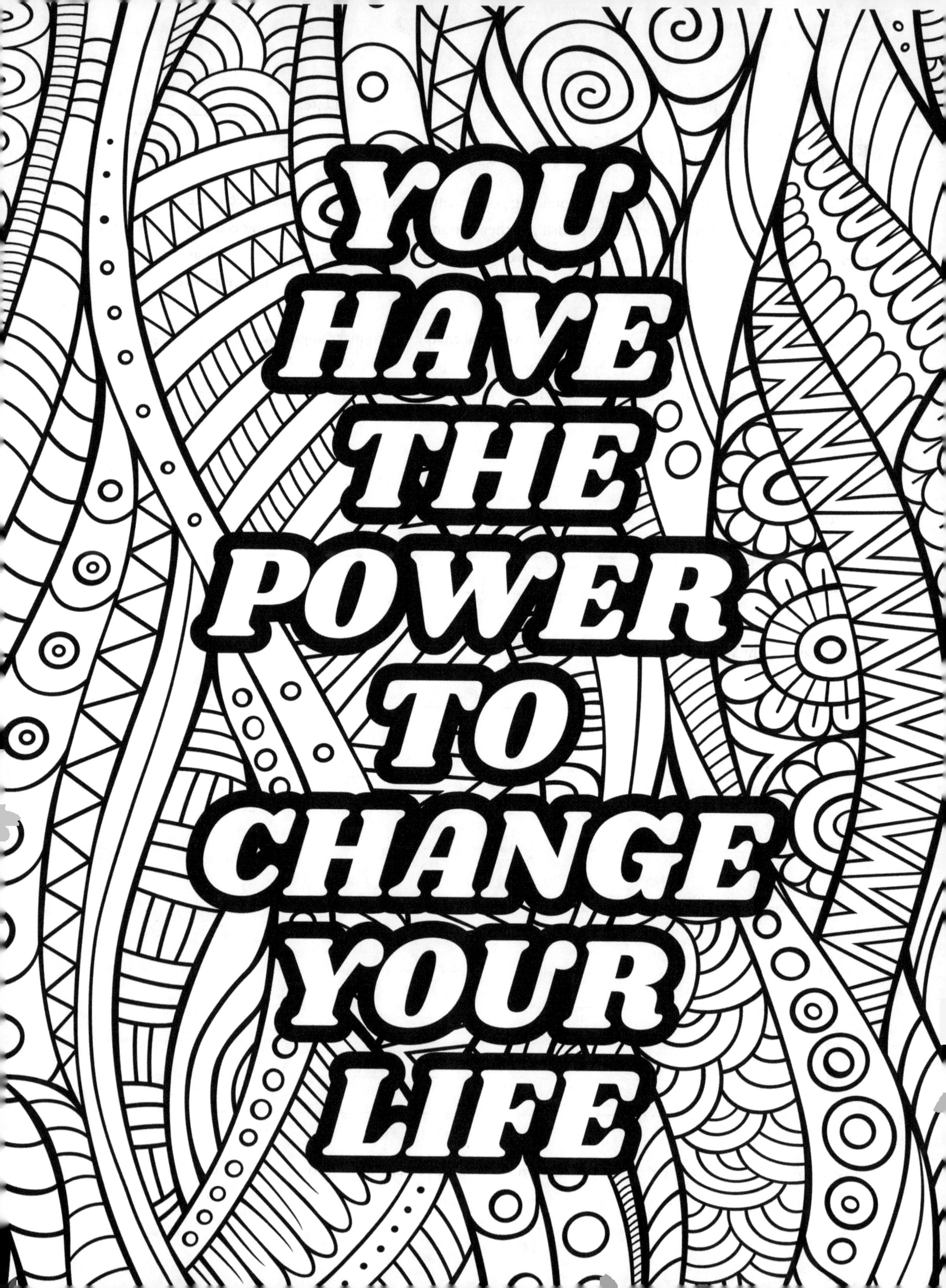
YOU
HAVE
THE
POWER
TO
CHANGE
YOUR
LIFE

Exercise 5: Implementing New And Healthy Habits

Many times, we get stuck in a routine and repeat a cycle of actions almost robot-like. In reality, life will never change if you keep on repeating the same patterns. Setting goals, creating plans, and taking small steps toward them can lead to remarkable achievements. With persistence and a positive mindset, each one of us can create a life that we desire and deserve. Therefore, it is essential to realize that the power lies within us, and we have complete control over our lives' direction.

Directions: In order to unlock the benefits that come with changing your life for the better, begin by outlining certain aspects of your life that you'd like to create new and healthy habits.

A new skill you'd like to learn:
_____

A topic you're going to master:
_____

A bad habit you're going to break:
_____

A country you'd like to visit:
_____

A language you want to learn:
_____

A new food you want to try:
_____

A good deed you're going to do:
_____

A successful person you're going to emulate:
_____

A book you'd like to read:
_____

A plant you're going to nurture:
_____

A place you'd like to live for a year:
_____

Takeaway: The more you begin to implement new patterns into your life, the higher the chances of *you* living your best life.

YOU HAVE OPTIONS AVAILABLE TO YOU

Exercise 6: What You Have Going For You

Sometimes our minds get stuck thinking that we have no options. However, this couldn't be further from the truth. Realistically, you _do_ have options available to you, but you're too focused on seeing the negative that you can't see the positive. When you're able to recognize the good stuff in life, it becomes easier to see that you're not completely backed into a corner with no way out.

Directions: Fill in the blanks below and pinpoint what you have going for you, plus who's on your side.

1) One achievement you have worked hard at:

_____

2) One area of your life that's thriving right now:

_____

3) Three professional industries you possess knowledge about:

    a) _____

    b) _____

    c) _____

4) Three people you can count on for good advice and encouraging words:

    a) _____

    b) _____

    c) _____

5) Three life events or moments you are looking forward to:

    a) _____

    b) _____

    c) _____

6) Two creative life pursuits you're passionate about exploring:

    a) _____

    b) _____

7) Two amazing talents you possess that can be turned into a side business:

    a) _____

    b) _____

Takeaway: You can do whatever you set your mind to!

LIFE SHOULD BE LIVED TO THE FULLEST

Exercise 7: Finding Your Purpose

Living life to the fullest and focusing on your life purpose is important because life is short and unpredictable. By focusing on your purpose, you align your actions and desires with your fundamental values, leading to a more fulfilling existence. Moreover, living life to the fullest involves taking risks, challenging yourself, making mistakes, and learning from them. These experiences enable you to grow as a person and develop a wealth of valuable life lessons. Without taking these risks and focusing on a purpose, life can become mundane, and the potential for growth and satisfaction can be diminished. Therefore, mindset is everything!

Directions: Write your answer below to the following prompt, hopefully it inspires you to live your best life.

If you had 1 year to live, with all the money in the world and access to anything you could possibly need, what goals would you accomplish, where would you travel to, and what would you do that you didn't think was possible before learning of your limited life expectancy?

_____

_____

_____

_____

_____

_____

_____

_____

Takeaway: Living life to the fullest and focusing on your life purpose allows you to make the most of your time on Earth and create a life that is truly meaningful to you.

NEVER STOP LEARNING

Exercise 8: Expanding Your Mind

We are constantly evolving as human beings. Our life experiences and the people we encounter teach us life lessons. While pursuing a higher education will always enable you to excel in the workforce and life in general, you don't need a college degree to prove your intelligence. Having the drive and ambition to absorb knowledge will take you very far in life. Therefore, regardless if you choose to enroll in an online course, attend a seminar, or take college classes, it's still valuable to pursue the truth for yourself.

Directions: Begin your quest and pursuit for knowledge by filling in the blanks below. **List 10 successful people, topics, subjects, or professions you want to learn more about:**

1) _____

2) _____

3) _____

4) _____

5) _____

6) _____

7) _____

8) _____

9) _____

10) _____

Takeaway: Now that you have a small list outlined, perform your own due diligence and begin learning more about each one of them in your free time. Google is a great teacher!

YOU WILL NEVER KNOW UNTIL YOU ASK

Exercise 9: Stepping Outside Of Your Comfort Zone

As humans, we tend to get comfortable in our daily routine and the thought of stepping out of our comfort zone can be daunting. However, it's important to remind ourselves that we can only grow when we are challenged. This mindset also applies to asking questions; we should never be afraid to ask for clarification or seek new knowledge. Whether it's in our personal or professional lives, stepping outside of our comfort zone and asking questions can lead to personal development, new opportunities, and a deeper understanding of the world around us. So embrace the uncertainty and take a chance, the rewards may surprise you.

Directions: Think of 6 pressing questions that are on your mind but you are too afraid to ask. Then, write them down and list who you plan to ask.

- Question 1:

  _____

  o   Who will you ask:

  _____

- Question 2:

  _____

  o   Who will you ask:

  _____

- Question 3:

  _____

  o   Who will you ask:

  _____

- Question 4:

  _____

  o   Who will you ask:

  _____

- Question 5:

  _____

  o   Who will you ask:

  _____

- Question 6:

  _____

  o   Who will you ask:

  _____

Takeaway: When you feel more confident, refer to this list of questions and ask the respective people what you've been wanting to know.

BE THANKFUL FOR WHAT YOU HAVE

Exercise 10: What You Have To Be Thankful For

Being grateful for what you have and giving thanks is essential to leading a happy and fulfilling life. By focusing on how you are blessed in your life, you become more appreciative and content. Expressing gratitude can also improve your relationships, as people are naturally drawn to those who are kind and thankful. So, take a moment to be grateful for everything you have, big or small.

Directions: Give thanks to what makes a positive impact on your life. Write your responses below.

List **5 people or pets** in your life that you're thankful for:

1) _____

2) _____

3) _____

4) _____

5) _____

List **5 life lessons** that you're thankful to have learned:

1) _____

2) _____

3) _____

4) _____

5) _____

List **5 joyful memories** that you're thankful to recall:

1) _____

2) _____

3) _____

4) _____

5) _____

Takeaway: We all lose sight of how blessed we are from time to time. Therefore, when you find yourself down on your luck, think of the people, pets, lessons, and memories you're thankful for.

BE THE BIGGER PERSON

Exercise 11: Understanding What Angers You

Taking the high road when you're angry is truly admirable because being the bigger person is easier said than done. It shows you can exhibit self control. Truth is, when anger gets a hold of you, it becomes very hard to think clearly and rationally. That's why it's crucial to understand your triggers and have coping skills to deal with anger before it affects your state of mind and well-being.

Directions: Answer the questions below and remember to apply these coping tools in real life.

1. Pinpoint the source of your anger. Sometimes we don't realize what triggers our anger until it's too late. That's why it's important to understand the source of your anger so you can consciously realize when a negative situation may arise. What makes you upset or triggers angry emotions within you?

a) _____

b) _____

c) _____

d) _____

e) _____

2. Figure out your coping skills. Being able to redirect your emotions from your trigger is key to calming your mind when you feel angry. What can you do – that brings you relief – in moments when your negative emotions might get the best of you?

a) _____

b) _____

c) _____

d) _____

e) _____

Takeaway: Once your mind gets clouded by anger, it becomes difficult to maintain self-control. However, when you are aware of your triggers and put safeguards in place like your personal coping skills to ease your frustrations, you become a stronger and more resilient version of yourself.

UNWIND AND ENJOY LIFE

Date: _____

Exercise 12: Pinpointing Your Stress Relief Outlets

It is crucial to manage worries if you want to enjoy life because excessive worrying can have a negative impact on mental and physical health. When we constantly focus on our worries, we become overwhelmed, stressed, anxious, and unable to enjoy life's precious moments. Furthermore, worrying can lead to a lack of sleep, lower energy levels, and decreased productivity, ultimately hindering our ability to live an enjoyable and fulfilling life. Therefore, it is necessary to learn to manage our worries and concerns by seeking help, adopting healthy coping mechanisms, and engaging in stress-relieving activities, as it enables us to live life to the fullest.

Directions: Circle the activities that you are curious about and enjoy doing.

Exercise

go for a walk   follow an exercise video

enjoy a bike ride   go for a swim

go to the gym   practice yoga

Socialize

call or text a friend   visit family

organize a group dinner   join a club or professional group

Responsibilities

clean or do housework   professional development

pay bills   do homework or study

Hobbies

play sports   go for a hike

enjoy gardening   play with a pet

draw or paint   enjoy cooking a meal

play music   catch up on your favorite show

Personal Care

get dressed up   prepare a healthy meal

get a haircut   tend to spiritual needs

Takeaway: Focusing on your worries is not healthy. When your mind is overcome with worries, take a moment to unwind and enjoy life by engaging in one of the activities you've identified above.

KEEP TRYING UNTIL YOU SUCCEED

Exercise 13: Your Achievable 6-Month Goal

It's very important to have goals and aim your efforts on achieving a particular desired result. Not only do goals imbue a sense of purpose, they also fill you with motivation, and give you a feeling of empowerment once you accomplish them. To add to that, setting goals helps you make significant strides and advancements as you navigate your life path.

Directions: Fill in the blanks below as you take into account your lifestyle, finances, career, love life, continuing education, and family life. This exercise will help you set a goal and figure out how to accomplish it in 6 months.

A goal you can attain within the next 6 months:

_____

The date you expect to accomplish your goal (i.e. 6 months from today):

_____

What motivates you to attain this goal?

_____

The 3 qualities that make you capable of achieving this goal.

    1) _____

    2) _____

    3) _____

What are the challenges you think you will encounter?

_____

What are the steps you need to take?

_____

What steps or research have you completed so far?

_____

What is currently pending in the process?

_____

Takeaway: You can achieve your dreams. All you have to do is set a goal and put in the work to attain it.

TREASURE EACH MOMENT

Exercise 14: Expressing Self-Gratitude

Sometimes we put too much pressure on ourselves to achieve goals, act a certain way, earn lots of money, and live a celebrity-like life. When you place more emphasis on what you haven't achieved or possessions you don't have, it becomes difficult to treasure each moment and live life to the fullest. To that point, it's critical to have gratitude for every waking day and everything you have attained thus far.

Directions: Write a gratitude letter to *yourself*. Below, outline or express why you appreciate where you are at this point in life. Express gratitude for all the positive things in your life – from people to experiences and anything else that brings you joy and elicits feelings of pride.

_____

_____

_____

_____

_____

_____

_____

_____

_____

_____

_____

Takeaway: Being grateful for who you are, and what you have to offer others and this world brings you closer to your authentic-self. When you can treasure the most precious aspects of what life has to offer, many of the trivial and mundane pursuits you place energy on won't seem as important.

SAVE YOUR ENERGY

Exercise 15: Nurturing Your Mind, Body, And Spirit

Being mindful of your mind, body, and spirit when getting defensive is crucial as it can help you understand the root cause of what's agitating you and how to manage it effectively. It is important to save your energy rather than acting defensively because defensiveness can lead to conflicts and misunderstandings. When we are defensive, we tend to focus on protecting ourselves and our beliefs, and may ignore or dismiss the other person's perspective. This can create an adversarial relationship and make it difficult to resolve the issue at hand. On the other hand, when we save our energy and approach a situation with an open mind and a willingness to listen and understand, we are more likely to find common ground and come to a mutually beneficial solution.

Directions: Complete this exercise. **When you begin to feel like you are about to get defensive:**

- How will you protect your mind?

_____

_____

_____

- How will you calm your body?

_____

_____

_____

- How will you nurture your spirit?

_____

_____

_____

Takeaway: Ultimately, being mindful of your mind, body, and spirit when getting defensive can enable you to live a more peaceful life. In the long run, saving your energy and being open to different perspectives can lead to stronger relationships and a more positive and constructive approach to problem-solving.

GO WITH THE FLOW

Exercise 16: Identifying The Source Of Your Stress

No one wants to feel stressed, but it happens. However, if you don't find ways to alleviate and manage stress, it can wreak havoc in your life. Stress affects our physical and mental health in various ways, including high blood pressure, anxiety, insomnia, and depression. It can lead to a decline in productivity and overall well-being. With that being said, stress management skills work by helping individuals recognize their triggers and learn how to manage them effectively. Techniques like deep breathing, exercise, and meditation are effective tools in managing stress. By incorporating stress management skills into our daily routine, we can improve our overall health, productivity, and happiness.

Directions: Find out your stress management needs by thoughtfully answering the questions below.

What makes me feel stressed?

_____

What do I gain from stress?

_____

What does feeling stressed take away from me?

_____

How does being stressed benefit me?

_____

How does stress negatively affect me?

_____

What stress management skills do I currently use?

_____

When I am stressed out, I feel...
(circle all that apply)

Anxious	Tense	Frustrated
Depressed	Upset	Panicked
Exhausted	Overwhelmed	Afraid
Alone	Insecure	Dizzy

Takeaway: Stress kills; that's why it's critical to understand how it affects you. And, now that you have a better understanding of what stress is doing to you – you can fix it.

MAKE
WISE
AND
INFORMED
DECISIONS

Exercise 17: Discovering Your Core Values

It's critical to develop core values that propel you forward throughout your lifetime. Being confident in yourself and the decisions you make is very liberating. It also demonstrates that you have a positive self-image and maintain a high self-worth. Without core values, it's difficult for a person to develop a strong sense of self, often leaving them vulnerable to negative influences. For instance, sometimes we overlook the consequences of our actions because we're having too good a time to care. Or, we find it difficult to say no because we want to feel accepted. However, when you feel empowered by your core values, you're less likely to make decisions that stray from those values.

Directions: Discover your core values by answering the questions presented below.

What are your values?

_____

_____

What is most important to you?

_____

_____

What do you want for your future?

_____

_____

What do you think the world needs?

_____

_____

When and why do you falter from your values?

_____

_____

How do you stay true to your values?

_____

_____

Takeaway: Think about your core values when you find yourself giving into temptation or anger.

Exercise 18: Gauging Your Self-Care Habits

Self-love is essential to fostering good mental health because it allows you to build a positive relationship with yourself. When you have a healthy sense of self-love, you are better able to manage stress and negative emotions, as well as prioritize your well-being. By acknowledging your strengths, celebrating your successes, and practicing self-compassion, you can boost your self-esteem and develop a more optimistic outlook on life.

Directions: One of the tell-tale signs of self-love is your ability to provide self-care. Assess your patterns.

Do you think self-care is important?

_____

_____

When you take care of yourself, how do you feel?

_____

_____

What is your favorite self-care activity?

_____

_____

What is your least favorite self-care activity?

_____

_____

What are some physical indicators that you need to make time to take care of yourself?

_____

_____

After you engage in a self-care activity, how do you feel?

_____

_____

As you review your answers to the questions above, how would you summarize your patterns for self-care on a scale from 1 to 5 (i.e. 1 = needs improvement, 2 = decent, 3 = average, 4 = good, 5 = excellent)?

_____

Takeaway: Self-love is crucial to fostering good mental health; it promotes a sense of self-worth and resilience, allowing you to navigate life's challenges with greater ease and confidence. Love yourself – you're worth it!

LEARN TO PRACTICE PATIENCE

Exercise 19: Conquering Your Triggers

Practicing mindfulness involves being aware of your thoughts, physical sensations, and emotions in the present moment without judgment. By doing so, you can identify triggers that make you angry and learn how to respond to them in a more constructive way. Furthermore, being mindful also helps you cultivate compassion and empathy for yourself and others, which can reduce the intensity and duration of your anger.

Directions: Complete the exercise below by filling in the blanks. First, start by listing your trigger like someone invading your personal space or cutting you off in traffic. Second, write your typical reaction to being in this scenario (i.e. "instead of flipping out"). Third, flip your response by saying what you will do instead (i.e. "I will take 2 steps back and stay calm).

List Your Trigger   Flip Your Response

When

_____

Instead of   I will

_____

When

_____

Instead of   I will

_____

When

_____

Instead of   I will

_____

When

_____

Instead of   I will

_____

Takeaway: Moving forward, be mindful of reacting too quickly when you grow impatient or become angry. Remember, you are in control of how you react to your triggers.

YOU ARE NOT ALONE

Exercise 20: What Are Your Go-To Mantras

Trauma, tragedy, and depression are often associated with feelings of loneliness and isolation because they can be incredibly overwhelming and tied to personal experiences. When we experience challenging circumstances, it can be difficult to comprehend or express what we are going through. Additionally, these experiences can create a rift between ourselves and others as we may feel like nobody can understand our pain or struggles. Moreover, trauma, tragedy, and depression can also result in isolation from society, often leading to a sense of being cut off from the world. This can create a vicious cycle of loneliness and mental health struggles where it seems impossible to connect with others or seek support.

Directions: Create 10 easy-to-remember mantras, slogans, or statements of what you need to remember when you feel overwhelmed, unacknowledged, anxious, depressed, or lonely. For example, *"I am not alone,"* *"This is a low moment and I will overcome it,"* or *"Don't give in, I am stronger than I give myself credit for."*

1) _____

2) _____

3) _____

4) _____

5) _____

6) _____

7) _____

8) _____

9) _____

10) _____

Takeaway: Negative emotions affect your ability to reason and think clearly. At some point in life, we all feel like no one understands what we are going through when in fact – you're not alone. Refer to these 10 mantras to help your mind refocus on statements that reinforce positive self-talk.

EVERY LITTLE BIT OF EFFORT COUNTS

Exercise 21: Being Proud Of Overcoming Adversity

Self-motivation is a powerful tool to keep persevering as it gives you the drive and determination you need to achieve your goals. When people are self-motivated, they do not need external sources of motivation to keep going. Instead, they rely on their own inner strength to keep pushing forward even in the face of setbacks, obstacles, or challenges. Additionally, self-motivation helps you to develop a positive mindset, adopt a "never give up" attitude, and maintain focus on your goals. As a result, you'll be more likely to persevere, overcome obstacles, and achieve success, both in your personal and professional life.

Directions: List 6 challenges you've overcome in your life, big or small. Then, write down why you are proud of yourself.

- Challenge 1:

    _____

    o Why are you proud of overcoming this challenge:

    _____

- Challenge 2:

    _____

    o Why are you proud of overcoming this challenge:

    _____

- Challenge 3:

    _____

    o Why are you proud of overcoming this challenge:

    _____

- Challenge 4:

    _____

    o Why are you proud of overcoming this challenge:

    _____

- Challenge 5:

    _____

    o Why are you proud of overcoming this challenge:

    _____

- Challenge 6:

    _____

    o Why are you proud of overcoming this challenge:

    _____

Takeaway: When you feel down on your luck, refer to this list to remind yourself of all the challenges you've overcome thus far.

TODAY IS A NEW DAY

Exercise 22: Making The Most Of Your Day

Each new day presents a chance to start over and improve yourself. Our past mistakes or failures do not define us, but rather help us learn and grow. With a new day comes new experiences and challenges that allow you to make better choices and decisions. It provides you with a fresh start to be the best version of yourself.

Directions: Learn to make the most of your day by putting genuine thought into your answers.

1. What does your ideal day look like?

   _____

2. How do you want to feel today?

   _____

3. What would make today wonderful?

   _____

4. What can you look forward to today?

   _____

5. What will you be great at today?

   _____

6. How can you make a difference today?

   _____

7. How can you be kind today?

   _____

8. How can you bring more peace into your life?

   _____

9. What has the potential to cause you stress or worry today, and how will you choose to respond to it?

   _____

10. How do you want to feel at the end of the day, and how can you make that a reality?

    _____

11. What emotional burden can you let go of today?

    _____

12. How will you care for yourself today?

    _____

13. What are you grateful for right now?

    _____

14. What good things are headed your way?

    _____

Takeaway: Each new day is a gift and it is up to you to make the most of it!

AIM FOR HIGHER GOALS

Exercise 23: Reaching For Your Biggest Goal

Reaching for higher goals in life provides numerous benefits. Firstly, it motivates you to focus on your personal growth and strive toward self-improvement, resulting in a sense of achievement and satisfaction. Secondly, pushing yourself to reach higher goals also encourages you to challenge your limits, leading to the development of new skills and abilities. Additionally, aiming for higher goals helps to broaden your perspective and enrich your experiences, allowing you to break out of your comfort zone and explore new opportunities.

Directions: Life is too short not to reach for the stars. Provide your answers below.

What is one *big goal* you think you will never achieve?

_____

Why do you think you won't fulfill this goal?

_____

_____

What do you need to achieve this goal?

_____

_____

Do you have the skills needed to attain this goal?

_____

_____

If you were to accomplish your big goal, how would you feel?

_____

If you weren't promised tomorrow, would you pursue your big goal?

_____

Takeaway: For a number of reasons, the human mind will place limitations upon itself and convince you that you are incapable of achieving certain goals. However, when you continuously reach for higher goals, you broaden your mind and open your life up to a plethora of possibilities.

FOSTER GOOD HEALTH

Exercise 24: Finding An Optimal You

It is essential to prioritize your health to balance emotions as it plays a crucial role in our overall well-being. A healthy lifestyle can help regulate emotions, improve mood, reduce stress and anxiety, and promote better sleep. When you prioritize your health by maintaining a balanced diet, regular exercise, and getting enough restful sleep, your body can produce endorphins, which are natural painkillers and mood boosters, leaving you feeling more relaxed and at ease. By cultivating a healthy lifestyle, you are not just taking care of your physical health but also your mental and emotional well-being, leading to a more balanced life and a happier you.

Directions: Answer the questions below and find clarity about how you can begin to achieve optimal health.

What activities, beauty treatments, and doctors do you rely on to keep up your physical health and appearance?

_____

What dietary changes can you implement to promote good health and foster emotional wellness?

_____

What sleep issues are you dealing with that should be discussed with your therapist or doctor?

_____

Why should you avoid ingesting mood-altering substances like alcohol and drugs, and not misuse prescription or over-the-counter medications?

_____

What actions or exercises will you do everyday to get enough physical activity?

_____

What can you do to improve how you treat your body? How will you incorporate it into your routine?

_____

What positive steps can you take for overall well-being?

_____

Takeaway: Most of us put aside taking care of our health because we prioritize everything else. We often forget that when our health suffers, so does our body, mind, and quality of life. That's why it's critical to foster good health.

REMAIN CALM AND FOCUSED

Exercise 25: How Anger Grabs Ahold Of You

It is important to remain calm and focused when you feel angry because anger often leads to irrational behavior and poor decision making. When we are angry, our emotions are heightened and we may say or do things that we later regret. Taking a step back, breathing deeply, and focusing on the situation at hand can help us process our emotions more effectively and find a solution that is rational and fair. Additionally, losing our cool can result in damaging relationships or creating greater conflict. By remaining calm and focused, we are more likely to resolve conflicts and maintain positive relationships with others.

Directions: Answer the questions posed below to gain a better awareness of how your anger presents itself.

When you are angry what do you feel in your body (i.e. tensing of muscles, grinding teeth, surges of energy through limbs, upset stomach, sweating, panting, etc.)?

_____

What do you want to do when you are angry?

_____

How do you usually react when angry (i.e. shouting, crying, shutting down, becoming physical by throwing or punching objects, becoming verbally or physically aggressive or violent with people, etc.)?

_____

Next time you are angry, how will you make sure you stay in control (i.e. walking away, deep breathing, rationalizing, contacting a supportive friend or family member, etc.)?

_____

What is the phrase you will use to remind yourself to stay in control?

_____

Takeaway: When anger grabs a hold of you, it can put you at risk for making poor decisions, or even worse, hurting others or yourself. That's why it is vital to know how you react when you are angry so that you can maintain control and be the bigger person.

DO NOT BE AFRAID TO SAY NO

Exercise 26: Personal Boundary Exploration

It is important to preserve one's sanity and boundaries by saying no when necessary. Saying yes to everything can result in burnout, exhaustion, and eventually, resentment. By setting limits and taking care of oneself, individuals can maintain a healthy balance between their personal and professional lives. Protecting one's boundaries is a way of respecting oneself and others. Saying no can also lead to better communication and honest relationships with others. Therefore, it is essential to say "no" when needed, to preserve one's well-being and maintain a healthy balance in life.

Directions: Circle the answer that best describes how often you experience each of the following scenarios.

1) You find it difficult to say "no" to people at work.
- All the time
- Sometimes
- Rarely
- Never

2) You find it difficult to say "no" to responsibilities.
- All the time
- Sometimes
- Rarely
- Never

3) You find it difficult to say "no" to family.
- All the time
- Sometimes
- Rarely
- Never

4) You find it difficult to say "no" to friends.
- All the time
- Sometimes
- Rarely
- Never

Takeaway: Now, you're aware of your patterns for saying "no" to certain people and can actively work on strengthening your response if need be.

BE A
LEADER
NOT
A
FOLLOWER

Exercise 27: Transforming Yourself Into A Leader

Leaders have the power to create positive change and inspire others to do the same. They are able to think critically, innovate, and take risks, which can lead to personal growth and success. Ultimately, being a leader means being in control of one's own destiny and making a difference in the world.

Directions: Everyone has leadership qualities within them. More so, those traits can be improved over time. Answer the questions below to find out more about your leadership path.

What is a leader?

_____

What traits and characteristics does a *leader* possess?

_____

What leadership qualities do *you* possess?

_____

How do effective leaders inspire others?

_____

What are your greatest strengths as a leader?

_____

How can you be a leader;
- at home

_____
- at work

_____
- in an academic setting

_____
- in your community

_____

Takeaway: It's not easy to lead, and it's even harder to lead with compassion. With that being said, you have the ability to help others, and if you can do it gracefully without instilling fear in others, it speaks volumes to the remarkable person you are.

DO WHAT MAKES YOU HAPPY

Exercise 28: Discovering Your Life Passion

You should do what makes you happy because life is too short to live in misery. Pursuing your interests and passions not only brings you joy and fulfillment, but it also helps you lead a more authentic and purposeful life. When you engage in activities that truly make you happy, you are more likely to perform better and feel more motivated, which can lead to greater success in every aspect of your life. Additionally, when you prioritize your own happiness, you inspire others to do the same and create a ripple effect of positivity in your community. So, do what makes you happy and live your life to the fullest.

Directions: Answer the questions below to find out what you are passionate about.

1. What is your dream life? Sum it up in 1 sentence.
    _____

2. What topics can you talk about all day without getting exhausted?
    _____

3. When are you the happiest?
    _____

4. What are you inspired by?
    _____

5. Who inspires you, living or from the past? Why?
    _____

6. What is 1 subject you can teach to an audience?
    _____

7. In an ideal scenario, would you rather work for yourself or for someone else?
    _____

8. What work would you do for free if money didn't matter?
    _____

9. If you could create a cure for something, what would it be?
    _____

10. If you could invent something, what would it be and what purpose would it serve?
    _____

11. If you could write a book, what would it be about?
    _____

12. If you could solve a global crisis, what would it be?
    _____

Takeaway: When you live a life with a sense of purpose, it makes life more enjoyable. That's why it's key to do what makes you happy and find ways to make your dreams come true.

MAKE SURE YOUR NEEDS ARE BEING MET

Exercise 29: What Are Your Non-Negotiables

Whether it's a romantic relationship, a friendship, or even a familial bond, there are times when we may find ourselves constantly giving and receiving little in return. This can leave us feeling depleted, unappreciated, and undervalued. Furthermore, it can also prevent us from building healthy boundaries. Therefore, it's important to recognize when a relationship is taking more than it's giving and take steps to either address the issue or let go of the connection altogether. Otherwise, we risk compromising our own emotional well-being and happiness.

Directions: Answer the following 7 questions to gain more insight into a few of your needs.

Name the people who take from you more than they give.

_____

What are 3 examples of what you consider to be an overstepping of your personal boundaries?

1) _____
2) _____
3) _____

What do you need in a romantic partner to feel secure?

_____

What are the characteristics and traits that you need your group of friends to possess?

_____

Name the people in your life who are negative influences or never have anything nice to say to you.

_____

What do you need from your employer in order to feel appreciated?

_____

What are 3 phrases you need to hear from the people you love?

1) _____
2) _____
3) _____

Takeaway: When you find yourself doubting whether certain relationships in your life are good for you, refer to your answers above to provide clarity.

MAKE IT HAPPEN FOR YOU

Exercise 30: Training Your Mind With Affirmations

You can achieve anything in life...with the right mindset. Positive affirmations are a powerful tool to improve mental health because they help to reprogram negative thought patterns and beliefs. By regularly repeating positive statements, you can reduce stress, anxiety, and depression. To add to that, positive affirmations can help to increase confidence, self-esteem, and empower individuals to make positive changes in their lives. When using positive affirmations, it releases endorphins and dopamine, which help boost self-motivation and create an overall sense of well-being. It is important to use positive affirmations to focus on the present moment, and not dwell on the past or worry about the future. Developing a habit of repeating positive affirmations can significantly improve your mental health and help you develop a positive outlook on life (and yourself).

Directions: List 10 positive affirmations about yourself below. For example, affirmations are "I" statements like "I am the bigger person," "I am resilient," or "I am authentic."

- Affirmation 1:

_____

- Affirmation 2:

_____

- Affirmation 3:

_____

- Affirmation 4:

_____

- Affirmation 5:

_____

- Affirmation 6:

_____

- Affirmation 7:

_____

- Affirmation 8:

_____

- Affirmation 9:

_____

- Affirmation 10:

_____

Takeaway: When negative thought patterns arise repeat your positive affirmations. They'll remind you of how amazing you are and that you can achieve anything you set your mind to!

BEGIN ON THE RIGHT FOOT

Exercise 31: Outlining Your Future Goals

Remaining productive throughout the day is an essential aspect of achieving success. Productivity enhances our efficiency, allowing us to tackle more tasks in less time and achieve more significant milestones. Consistent productivity builds positive habits that enable us to create a solid work ethic, increased self-discipline, and a robust sense of achievement.

Directions: Complete the questions below to identify your short-term, long-term, and life goals.

Short-Term Goals

- What are your goals for this month?

  _____

- What are your goals for the next 3 months?

  _____

Long-Term Goals

- What goals do you want to accomplish within the next year?

  _____

- Where do you see yourself 5 years from now, and 10 years from now?

  _____

Life Goals

- What kind of life do you imagine having? Describe it and what's missing.

  _____

- What needs to change or improve so you can live the lifestyle you desire?

  _____

- How do you plan on attaining this lifestyle? What's your plan of action?

  _____

Takeaway: Remaining productive throughout the day sets us up for success by ensuring that we are continuously taking action toward our goals. All you have to do is take active steps toward executing your plan.

ABOUT THE AUTHOR & BRAND

AVNI PAREKH

A dynamic award-winning author, entrepreneur, and TV personality, Avni's resume is nothing short of impressive. Her self-help book, *Be The Bigger Person: Scenarios & Solutions to Better Yourself,* was named a Winner of the 2023 Human Relations Indie Book Awards and a Finalist of the 2023 Book Excellence Awards. Avni's books about self-discovery and personal growth are written with the intention of inspiring readers to overcome life's obstacles with grace and reach their full potential.

THE BRAND

BE THE BIGGER PERSON is more than just a slogan, it's a life principle and way of life. "Be the bigger person" means taking the high road when faced with difficult situations and interpersonal conflicts, without resorting to violence. Avni's mindful brand branches out into several different industries, all while staying true to its core values.

MINDFUL APPAREL

Avni's merchandise includes size-inclusive, unisex athleisure, as well as hats, mugs, and more. Near and dear to Avni's heart are the messages showcased on the apparel which highlight fundamental aspects of *Be The Bigger Person, Don't Give In,* and *I'm Above It*!

#BTBP CAMPAIGN

#BTBP or #bethebiggerperson is a universal campaign to remind folks to choose the high road in life, rather than succumb to anger when faced with negativity. Use these hashtags on social media to convey your words of encouragement and stories of overcoming adversity.

FOLLOW ON SOCIAL

We're on Instagram, Facebook, and Twitter under the handles:
@BTBPbook and @AvniParekh

---

www.BTBPshop.com

GET THE MERCH

Our Mindful Apparel Helps Reinforce Key Messages
Like Be The Bigger Person, Don't Give In,
I'm Above It & More!

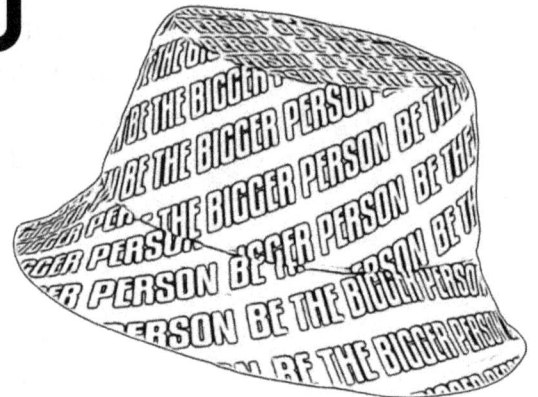

www.BTBPshop.com

ABOUT THE COLLECTION

1. SELF-HELP BOOK

2. COLOR-IN WORKBOOK

3. COLORING BOOK

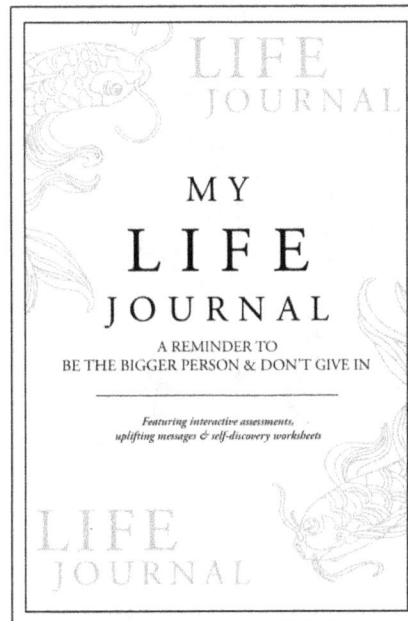

4. HANDS-ON JOURNAL

FREE DOWNLOAD

DIG INTO YOUR SUBCONSCIOUS MIND

READER'S GUIDE

SCAN ME

SCAN ME

SCAN ME

SCAN ME

Discover the ultimate path to personal growth with the complimentary Reader's Guide for award-winning self-help book *Be The Bigger Person*, which includes a specially-curated questionnaire composed by the author herself. Unleash your potential and unlock the keys to self-improvement as you delve deeper into the book's transformative concepts and practical strategies.

This comprehensive guide serves as your personal roadmap, guiding you through each chapter with insightful prompts and thought-provoking exercises. Embrace a journey of self-discovery, understanding, and empowerment as you reflect on your values, beliefs, experiences, and aspirations. Avni Parekh's expertise and compassionate approach will empower you to overcome challenges, cultivate resilience, and foster authentic connections with others.

Take your personal growth to new heights! Download the complimentary Reader's Guide now and embark on your transformative quest to become the bigger person you've always aspired to be.

YOU HAVE REACHED THE END OF THIS BOOK
A TRANSFORMED VERSION OF YOURSELF - CONGRATS!
DON'T GIVE IN & NEVER GIVE UP

www.ingramcontent.com/pod-product-compliance
Lightning Source LLC
Chambersburg PA
CBHW062108090426
42741CB00015B/3360